Traces of Eden: Travels in the Desert Southwest

Traces of Eden: Travels in the Desert Southwest

PHOTOGRAPHS BY MARK KLETT

ESSAY BY DENIS JOHNSON

CRITICAL TEXT BY PETER GALASSI

A POLAROID BOOK ✢ DAVID R. GODINE, PUBLISHER, INC. ✢ BOSTON

First edition published in 1986 by
David R. Godine, Publisher, Inc.
Horticultural Hall
300 Massachusetts Avenue
Boston, Massachusetts 02115

This book was prepared and produced by the Publications Department of Polaroid Corporation.

Library of Congress Catalog Card Number 85-82074
ISBN 0-87923-617-5

First edition
Printed in the United States of America

COVER: Beneath the Great Arch, near Monticello, Utah, 6/21/82

BORDER OF SIGHT

DENIS JOHNSON

On the southwestern deserts the nights are clear over the highways. It is a major temptation to drive with the lights off. It is impossible to move through this vision without becoming aware again that we've been given the gift of sight.

The first nuclear explosion happened in the American Southwest, in New Mexico. When they witnessed the rising of this sun they had created, many of the people working on the project began running toward it, overcome by something like the desire to offer worship. Oppenheimer later reported telling himself, "Now physicists have known sin." But Victor Weisskopf said he thought instantly, as he watched the orange fireball levitating amid its electric-blue halo, "of Grünewald's Christ ascending in the *Resurrection*."

Over the last forty years the American Southwest has absorbed atomic blasts equal to one-sixth the megatonnage projected for the thermonuclear holocaust of which we live in dread.

The Southwest isn't all desert. Natural garden parks follow one another from the Idaho mountains down one river after another and into Mexico.

There is plenty of water in the Southwest – lakes and streams abound, and the citizens of Arizona own, per person, the largest number of boats of any state in the nation – but there isn't much water in the air.

Where only a little rain falls, the land keeps its level, shifted but not very much eroded or essentially changed by the winds, while the water of rivers cuts deeper and deeper into the world – thus the southwestern canyons: the Whirlpool Canyon on the Green River in northeastern Utah; and on the Colorado into which it feeds, Still-

water, Cataract, and Glen canyons; and then Marble Canyon, the Echo Cliffs, and the Grand Canyon in Arizona. On the Virgin River in Nevada, the Paranuweap Canyon is in places only twenty feet wide but a thousand feet deep. The canyons of the arid places are numberless.

These fissures, many full of violent water, and many others as dry and silent as the bones that lie in them, and still others sleeping now under man-made reservoirs, are the secrets of the horizons. They aren't visible to a person standing on one of the highways to Las Vegas, perhaps stranded out of gas, or simply stretching his legs, or pulling a trigger just to feel the power of gunfire as it shreds a two-centuries-old saguaro cactus, and just to hear the desert eat the noise.

The Colorado River was said by the Indians to have been laid out by God as a highway to Heaven for a man who refused to stop mourning for his wife until he'd seen her in that place. When the man came home, comforted to have seen his wife in the afterworld, God filled this road to Paradise with maelstroms and drowning in order to keep others from going there. Now we can gather that the widower stands, slightly drunk and unhappy with his car's radiator, out of sight of the Colorado River, on the road to the capitals of gambling and divorce and the tumbling rapids of money turning over and over.

The canyons are the clear record of the past, the highways the clear record of the present. The future stands changeless and eternal in the desert and the ranges. But like the future, the belittling stasis of mountains can be crossed. And we cross, it seems, unable not to. What we seek refuge from so desperately is the future, and the only method we have for escaping the future is to move into it and claim it as the present. This is the great endeavor of the West.

The canyons of the Green and the Colorado rivers were first mapped by John Wesley Powell in 1869. From Powell's journal it would appear that his band of explorers spent a great deal of their time and made a good bit of their distance by carrying their cargo, and often even their boats, overland beside waters too rough to accommodate any passage.

Powell's party had reason to be cautious because, according to their best information, the Colorado poured into a hole in the earth somewhere in Arizona and rushed for an unknown distance through a void.

They began their journey at Green River City in what is now Wyoming. Within two weeks, within the first fifty miles, they had a boat dashed to pieces on the rocks of the Canyon of Lodore rapids. The three men in the boat made it safely to an island in the river's midst, from which the rest of the party rescued them. The three were lost and then recovered all in the space of a few minutes, but "We are as glad to shake hands with them," Powell wrote that night in his diary, "as though they had been on a voyage around the world, and wrecked on a distant coast."

The next day, a little way downriver, they came on the wreckage of the first party of white people ever to try this journey.

As Powell had it, hardly anything was known about those first explorers except that they were led by a man named Ashley. Some miles above the place of these disasters, the name Ashley can be read where he chiseled it into a rock, along with the date, which is illeg-ible. Shortly afterward, according to Powell, almost everyone in the Ashley party was killed. Ashley and one other man climbed from the waters alive, and hauled themselves up the canyon's walls. Living on berries and cactus they made their way overland to Salt Lake City, took refuge with the Mormons, and earned their way by laboring on the foundation of the temple. Powell couldn't find anyone to tell him what became of Ashley and his nameless companion after they left that town.

But Powell was listening to local legend. In truth it's doubtful that the Ashley who carved his name onto a rock and then wrecked his party in the Green River ever saw the temple, or even its foundation, in Salt Lake City. A William Henry Ashley, who eventually became a congressman for Missouri, is credited with having navigated the Green River in 1825 and with establishing fur-trade routes in that country that made him a rich man; and in 1826 he led an expedition that reached the vicinity of the Great Salt Lake. He died in 1838. The Mormons, on the other hand, didn't establish their colony in Salt Lake until decades later: in the late 1840s, without a map, a stream of some twelve thousand apostles of Brigham Young – a New Englander with some twenty-seven wives and scores of children – crossed the world from Nauvoo, Illinois. The first of them arrived in the summer, exhausted and starved, near the endless burning white flats of the Great Salt Lake, the country of distance, light, and dreams, leaving in their wake four relay colonies and more than two thousand graves.

At that time Utah was a part of Mexico, forsaken by the American people and also, according to the mountain men who had first reached her, forsaken by God. Here, in the Salt Lake Valley, a full thousand miles beyond what had been, until then, the farthest American frontier, the Mormons settled down to build their temple and lay out a celestial city and await, as they continue to do, the destruction of the world by fire.

Parts of the desert, in themselves forbidding, are also forbidden: areas of the Nellis Bombing and Gunnery Range Complex in Nevada are off limits, especially Yucca and Frenchman Flats, the two dry lake beds where from 1951 to the early sixties America exploded its atomic weapons; in Utah, the Dugway Proving Grounds, the Hill Air Force Range, the Windover Range, and the Desert Test Center are all restricted; and much of Edwards Air Force Base on the Mojave in California – where the sound barrier fell in 1947 and the Space Shuttle *Columbia* touched down in 1981 – is closed to us; and south of Death Valley, the roads to the China Lakes Naval Weapons Center and the Fort Irwin Military Reservation are barred. On the Sonoran Desert in Arizona, sixteen Titan II missiles bearing nuclear warheads are planted in a kind of circle of power around the city of Tucson. These are things the maps might tell you, or the newspapers. The people of the Mojave will tell you you're getting close to the Nevada line and that you can wander at seventy m.p.h. up Interstate 15 through Nipton and other towns without grass – towns made out of trailers and stunned by heat – to Las Vegas, a city that cherishes several green lawns and some trees and seems to take place in an enormous silence, like a phonograph playing in the wilderness. Even indoors the games clink and whir irrelevantly within the larger pursuit of time going after endlessness. Las Vegas is not forbidding. It's an inviting town; in fact it's a town that's hard to get out of. And yet it's a simple matter to walk after dark down the Strip to the border of neon and, whether you're a winner or a loser, to stare at a blackness that seems to reach down into the heart of all experience.

Other places seem forbidding or forsaken but are neither. Near the waterless Gila River in Arizona, a dozen miles from the trailer-town (population twenty) of Sentinel, a mile past the ghost town of Agua Caliente (a main street, a collapsing two-storied hotel, and sand-drifted storefronts snagged with tumbleweed, once a small resort until the hot springs one day ceased) past these, a pie-shaped tin sign on a phone pole announces *The Children of Light/Three Mi.* and points down a dirt path through a slag-heap dreamscape of asteroidal desolation. The air along this one-lane path, and the atmosphere over Agua Caliente and over Sentinel, is a perpetually shimmering fog of dust out of which now appears a metal corral-gate hung with another sign: *Welcome/ Kindly Shut/ Gate Behind You.*

Beyond this gate the world is altered. Suddenly the path is walled and roofed with date palms fifty feet tall. Crimson and yellow and pale blue rose bushes, oleanders, and morning glories pour up out of their roots. The mild, ceaseless desert dust-blow falls here, too, but now it comes down through the rainbow mist of sprinklers and descends on a number of low buildings and green lawns attended by venerable gnarled pine trees, and on a motel-sized swimming pool. Truck gardens and small fruit orchards lie around the buildings. In the middle of each garden, a faucet planted in the dirt spills clear water all day long, bringing it up unreasonably out of the heart of one of the most arid regions in the world and bestowing it on the shoots and seedlings of the Children of Light.

The Children of Light are not children. Most of them appear to be in their seventies. They are the Elect, living as virgins and eunuchs in the Reign of Heaven, and they do not expect to die. There are nineteen of them – a dozen women and seven men. They grow their own food, raise their own buildings, and make most of their clothes out of white linen imported from Scotland. They offer nothing for sale and solicit no contributions. Each one has taken the name of a stone.

When I visited them in 1981 I found their leader, Opal, a tall woman in her late seventies, tearing turnips up out of the earth in one of the gardens. On her vest of white linen her identification was embroidered in gold thread: *Elect Opal*. She wore a denim skirt and tennis shoes and the sweat poured off her. "It'll be time for water soon," she told me. I wondered why she didn't just stoop down and drink from the faucet two yards away, but I didn't ask. These people were inhabiting the elements of distance, light, and dream. I knew that nothing I knew applied here.

Elect Opal took me around the buildings, glad to entertain a visitor, and showed me how the basements were shelved and rowed with two- and three-gallon jugs of canned fruit and vegetables, grains, nuts, and dry beans. Their main business was to grow and stockpile this food. They already had enough to feed the nineteen of them for several decades. The Children of Light, she told me, were entirely self-sufficient and would continue to be so following the destruction of the world by fire. She didn't think highly of the descendants of Brigham Young and his followers. "The Mormons are storing up just for themselves," she said. "Our food supply is for anybody who finds us."

The Children of Light had begun, under Opal's leadership, in Canada some thirty years before. They had lost their church and had wandered for twelve years through the central provinces and down through the United States, in a caravan of cars and trailers, seeking their place and praying for deliverance from this vagabondage. "One night," she told me proudly, "in a location in Florida, I was sitting out front of the trailer with Jewel, and there did appear before us in the air a flaming television screen ringed around with a halo of purple fire. In the middle of the screen we both read these words: *Agua Caliente*. We found it on a map and came here."

Near the largest building, a dinner bell rang.

"It's time for water now," she said.

We went into the central building, a place with a roomy, modern kitchen, a dining area like a small cafeteria, and at the end opposite the kitchen, a plate glass window looking out on an arrangement of flowerbeds. Before the window was a kind of orchestra pit with a bass viola, a piano, some horns in their cases, and several music stands. "We have music on Sunday," Opal told me.

I greeted the others – speechless, smiling old women in white linen, and a few men who also had nothing to say to me – and we sat down to have water. We drank it measured out by the half-cup, because, Opal told me, somewhere in the Bible it says, "And they shall drink water by the measure." Every two hours Elect Phil, the only one not named for a mineral of the earth, rang the bell; and they all drank water together in the kitchen, by the measure.

Water is the heart of the miracle of the Children of Light. On their arrival in the town of Agua Caliente they found the empty hotel and the two dead streets and learned from the few residents of Sentinel, twelve miles away, that the hot springs had dried up, there had never been any fresh water, and nobody could hope to survive a summer here. The Children of Light camped out in the old hotel, and with pooled funds, under the direction of God and the guidance of Opal, they bought eighty acres of black slag, using their last few hundred dollars to hire a driller to go down a hundred feet for water. The driller got nothing. They asked him if he'd please go down another hundred feet without payment. He agreed, and several feet lower tapped into a buried lake of fresh water more massive than the acreage above it. It hadn't been there before. The construction of the Roosevelt Dam, two hundred miles away, had somehow caused the formation of this underground reservoir sometime in the previous five years.

It was Holy Saturday, and I'd come here to the easternmost fingertip of the Yuma Desert, four days after the Space Shuttle *Columbia*'s landing on the Mojave, to see if I might help the Children of Light greet this Easter. But they told me that celebrations and holidays were never observed here. Each morning, afternoon, and evening was the same in the Reign of Heaven.

Elect Topaz, a tiny, round old lady with a sweet, befuddled expression, told me that each morning before breakfast they got together in the basement right below our feet to pray and receive their instructions. After breakfast they labored through the day, sewing, canning, carpentering, hoeing, planting – water every two hours; lunch; dinner. They passed the evenings talking or reading. Sometimes there was music.

"Who gives you the day's instructions?" I asked.

"The Voice."

"The Voice?" I said. "Where does The Voice come from?"

"From Opal," she told me, "out of Opal's mouth."

After water, Opal showed me around the main building. The sewing room, housing half a dozen electric-powered Singers, was off the dining area. Beyond the kitchen, in another wing, we looked into the men's dormitory – rustic and wood-paneled – and the women's, which was done in a kind of pink French Provincial. There were private bedrooms, lavatories, a study, a sitting room of meditative quiet.

Upstairs was a room they never entered. "The Voice," Opal said, "asked us to build this." It was a fair-sized room with a fireplace, gleaming oak floors, and a tremendous table of cherry wood silently addressed by thirteen chairs. "We don't go in there," she said.

On the table a Bible – by far the largest book I'd ever seen, bigger than a whole case of most Bibles – lay spread open, but I never found out to what page.

"What is the purpose of this room?" I asked her.

She was amused by my question. "We don't know about any purposes," she said. "We were told to build it and we built it. Then The Voice said we'd better come up with a table and thirteen chairs. You have no idea the trouble we had getting that table built, getting it all the way out to this place, and then hauling it up here to the second floor." She pointed to our left, where they'd built a ramp from the ground up to this level. "It was the only way we could bring that table up here."

"This Voice," I said. "It just comes out of you all of a sudden?"

"Yes, it does," she said. "It's a great gift." Opal wasn't without a sense of humor. She seemed to be getting a kick out of my discomfort.

As I was leaving, Opal gave me a rose blossom, almost the size of a cabbage, in which four or five pastel colors swam together. "This is called a Joseph's Coat," she said. "The coat of many colors." She gave me a cake of heavy bread mixed with dates, nuts, and honey, which she referred to as "manna" – "They were given manna in the wilderness," she quoted for me. Dust fell down all over everything.

I said goodbye to Sapphire, a woman in her teens, the youngest of the Elect, and to Topaz, who'd apparently adopted her. "How do you choose your names?" I wanted to know.

"Oh," Sapphire said, "The Voice gives them to us," and Topaz nodded and said, "The Voice."

The Southwest is the only place on the earth with such a concentration of frightening names: Disaster Falls, Desolation Canyon, Dirty Devil River, Truth or Consequences, Flaming Gorge, Bad Land Cliffs, Devil's Playground, Massacre Lake, *Jornada del Muerto*, *Sangre de Cristo*, Death Valley, Skull Valley, Fool Creek, Tombstone . . .

Many of the landmarks along the Green and Colorado rivers were christened by John Wesley Powell. Some have kept their Indian names, and others have become what the Spanish priests or early settlers called them. A few have been officially redesignated: *Toompin Tuweap* (Land of Rock) is now Canyonlands National Park, Utah; Gunnison's Crossing has disappeared from the maps; and in Cataract Canyon, originally named by Powell, there are no more cataracts – at present it lies under the man-made body of water named for him, Lake Powell.

In his explorations, Powell learned that the Ute Indians weren't the first to live along the Green River. He located the foundations of ancient buildings and unearthed shards of pottery. The Utes knew of rocks, farther up the mountains, covered with pictures, but they had no idea who had made these things.

In Arizona, too, the dwellers first encountered by white explorers weren't themselves the first to dwell there. Some other civilization had preceded them, faded, and left no history. Its most extensive bequest to us is a great adobe structure surrounded by the remains of outbuildings, a sacred complex that stands within sight of the two water towers of the Arizona State Prison Complex in Florence. The huge adobe ruins facing the prison is called *Casa Grande*, the Big House, named without irony by the Papago Indians who discovered it centuries ago, the phrase later translated by the Spanish fathers. The people who erected the Big House are called *Hohokam*, "Those Who Are Gone." The name they gave to themselves, the name they had every reason to believe was their name, is forgotten.

What I'm getting at is that there is something essentially speechless, deaf, pure, and unendurable about this landscape. The mesas, mountains, and lakes hear nothing. The rivers don't hear their names.

The mountains are serene and beautiful, and the rivers are alive; but something under the desert speaks to the yearning spirit, chiefly by refusing to speak at all. In the immenseness of sand that goes on communing with itself in a terrifying way, ignoring everything, answering itself with itself while the sky overhead wears out, the soul feels the same insignificance as the soul of the lost sailor.

To a man or woman trying to get across it, it isn't a landscape but a hostile medium, a dusty and sometimes steamy glare of fortnights to the west, a hopeless waste very like the top of the sea, a place not so much to be looked at as lived through. Part of its beauty is this hard fact, that while we're seeing it, we're also surviving it.

Its look has been compared to the moon's, and the similarity is more than a visual one. Like the moon, the desert can't possibly be survived – but it has been. Like the moon, the desert is the place of distance, light, and dreams.

Art may imitate nature, but the artist is hard put to do what nature sometimes does. The desert does it simply by its austerity and hostility, the rivers by their obliviousness and violence, the mountain ranges by a senseless purposiveness that seems to have come with them up out of the earth. When the artist accomplishes it, the frame doesn't make a window; it makes an eye. It isn't the border of a picture, but the border of sight; and the sight arouses in us the humble gratitude of refugees.

Pausing to drink, Peralta Creek trail, Superstition Mtns, AZ, 1/8/83

Pause to drink

Spiral carving facing east, Signal Hill, 5/7/83

Spiral carving from .... rt   ....

Car passing snake, eastern Mojave Desert, 5/29/83

Car passing snake   eastern Mojave desert   5/19/83

"Paul and Edna," boulder near House Rock, Arizona, 9/14/83

"Paul and Edna" Gould "House Rock" Arizona 8/14/83

Campsite reached by boat through watery canyons, Lake Powell, 8/20/83

Campsite reached by boat through watery canyons.   Lake Powell 8/20/83

Plywood Tee-Pees, Meteor Crater, AZ, 5/30/82

Plywood Tee-Pees   Meteor Crater, AZ   5/30/82

Fallen cactus, new golf course, Pinnacle Pk, 3/4/84

Rock uplifted and shattered, Phoenix, Squaw Peak, 12/18/83

Rock uplifted and shattered   Phoenix   Squaw Peak 12/18/83

Tripod left on rock made from drifted sand, West Canyon, 9/14/84

Tripod left on rock ... from ... West Canyon

Bullet-riddled saguaro, near Fountain Hills, 5/21/82

Bullet riddled saguaro   near Fountain Hills 5/24/82

Stephanie walking a ledge above the Valley of Fire, Nevada, 5/28/84

Stephanie walking a ledge above the Valley of Fire   Nevada 5/28/84

Man behind creosote bush, Phoenix, 3/7/82

Desert marker, near Usery Mtn., 9/2/84

Desert marker   near Usery Mtn.   9/2/84

Kem Brown in her garden, Gimlet, Idaho, 9/6/81

Kem Brown in her garden   Gimlet, Idaho   9/6/81

Linda photographing the Petrified Forest, Arizona, 6/10/83

Linda photographing the Petrified Forest   *Arizona 6/10/83*

Truck moving west, Echo Cliffs from route 89A, AZ, 9/14/83

Truck moving west   Echo Cliffs from route 89A, Az 9/14/83

MARK KLETT:

PRESENT AND PAST IN THE AMERICAN WEST

PETER GALASSI

It is sometimes thought that the great nineteenth-century photographers of the American West did such fine work because they had such a hard time doing it. Their equipment was cumbersome, their materials demanding and fragile, and their transportation unreliable and slow. One may suppose but cannot always prove that in addition their food was primitive, their entertainment rare, and their women at home. Under such burdens and sacrifices, it is said, the photographers refused to tolerate aesthetic imprecision. They had gone too far to bring back mediocre pictures.

Some of us may balk at the implication that Timothy O'Sullivan or William Henry Jackson were good simply because they were tough, or at the notion that hard work inevitably must lead to good pictures. But there may be some truth to this claim. How else are we to explain the nearly universal success of the old photographers of the West? Not all of their pictures are as bold and graceful as the best efforts of O'Sullivan, but even the run of the mill is something that any photographer could have made with pride.

Few people are better equipped to judge this issue than Mark Klett. In 1977 Klett, fellow photographer JoAnn Verburg, and Ellen Manchester, a historian of Western photography, conceived a scheme of remaking the photographs of O'Sullivan, Jackson, and their colleagues. To be more precise, the idea was to execute a series of new photographs, each made from exactly the same viewpoint and under the same conditions of light and weather as the century-old original. After a few false starts the team assembled for this project perfected a method for doing just that. Between 1977 and 1980, Klett and the rest of the team remade no less than 122 of the old views, under the banner of The Rephotographic Survey Project (RSP). It was for

this project that Klett began using Polaroid Positive/Negative Land Film Type 55. The instant print was indispensable for on-site comparison with the nineteenth-century prototype, and a negative was required for later enlargements. Klett became "hooked on the stuff" and has continued to use the film for his own work.

All of O'Sullivan's and many of Jackson's western views were made for the United States geological surveys and were conceived, if not as scientific documents, at least as geological illustrations. This technical aspect of the pictures is mysterious and arcane to most of us, but not to Klett, who earned his undergraduate degree in geology. (He must be the only photographer for whom a fossil is named: the horseshoe crab *Casterolimulus kletti*, which Klett unearthed on a geological survey in North Dakota in 1973.) Although Klett no longer practices geology, his training helps us to understand the character of his photographs, which measure time not only in hours and days but also in centuries and millenia.

I remember thinking when I first met Mark Klett, just before the RSP work began, that the idea was a trifle nutty. I also suspected that he and Ellen Manchester, both Easterners by birth, had dreamed up the project as a pleasant way of paying homage to their adopted landscape and to the photographers they most admired. Certainly no one guessed at the time how absorbing and instructive the results would be. There was a faint expectation that the new photographs would reveal appalling disfigurations of the landscape: highways, motels, tourist traps, and the like. These predictable signs of decline turned out to be rare. Instead there appeared in the pictures a thousand fascinating and unpredictable clues to the nature of the landscape, the character of photography, and the methods of the old photographers. In the end Klett and his colleagues realized a historian's dream: Searching out the old views, measuring them against an infinity of rejected opportunities, the modern photographers came as close as one can imagine to experiencing the working life of their nineteenth-century predecessors. In the process some of the tough-guy myths evaporated – it appeared, for example, that most of the old photographs had been made not far from the trail – but the admiration remained, and deepened.

For Klett the RSP was more than a satisfying piece of work. It focused his ambitions as a photographer and it opened up for him the artistic territory he has been exploring so fruitfully ever since. From home bases in Colorado, Idaho, and Arizona he has covered great stretches of the West, photographing along the way. In this new work, illustrated here, the motive of the Survey Project persists: to measure the present against the past. But freed of the Project's confining definition, Klett now pursues this theme with flexibility and imagination, even playfulness.

Consider the picture titled *Campsite reached by boat through watery canyons*, *Lake Powell, 8/20/83*. The subject is not a natural wonder (as one might suppose) but a man-made lake, created by damming the Colorado River. In what some might regard as a painful irony, the lake is named for the great geologist John Wesley Powell, the first to explore the river. Klett does not explicitly refer to the history of the site, except in so far as his view recalls O'Sullivan's photographs of the Colorado, in which he often included his boat, named *Picture*. These photographs were made in 1871, the year in which Powell led his second expedition down the river. Perhaps Klett also remembered the celebrated story of O'Sullivan's hair-raising adventure on the rapids of Nevada's Truckee River in 1867. (This is not unlikely, since O'Sullivan had been on his way to photograph Pyramid Lake, which Klett rephotographed in 1979.) If Klett did remember, he doubtless appreciated all the more the safety and convenience of his motor-powered fiberglass boat, the focus of his picture.

In other pictures, Klett includes his VW Bug or his down sleeping bag or his lightweight plastic water bottles. Surely he means us to note the modernity of these things, as if the century separating them from O'Sullivan's crusty equipment were a long time. But always this message is framed generously by the landscape – imperceptibly different from O'Sullivan's – for which a century is almost nothing. All the same the viewer does not feel overwhelmed by the weight of geological history. It is one of the constant pleasures of Klett's pictures that irreconcilable scales of time find themselves in peaceful accord. (Only in a few recent pictures has Klett begun to test the potential of a deliberately jarring note.) Perhaps this harmony of time is partly a function of the spatial scale, which is broad but not vast, which acknowledges but does not insist on the smallness of man.

O'Sullivan's boat, his wagon, his second camera: when these shards of evidence appear in his pictures, historians eagerly magnify them for study, all the more eagerly because they are rare. In Klett's pictures even if we do not see the photographer's gear, the trace of man is never absent. Sometimes it is the graffiti of the ancient Indians (or of modern tourists); sometimes the figure of another hiker (or only his shadow). Instead of a perfect, monumental cactus, which O'Sullivan or Edward Weston would have presented as a triumph of nature, Klett shows us a weary veteran of target practice. And in a broad vista of sun-parched cliffs, the picture is bisected not only by a shadow but also by a highway. On it a truck travels west, blurred by speed.

For contemporary photographers of the West this strategy has become an indispensable sign, and sometimes a brazen badge, of honesty. It is felt that a picture of pristine nature would be in effect a lie, a coverup for the ugly marks modern man and especially modern commerce have left on the land. Klett obviously subscribes to this creed, but he has escaped the bitterness or routine complaint that often goes with it.

Careful inspection of Klett's view at Meteor Crater, Arizona, or a quick glance at its title, will reveal that the tepees are made of plywood, set up as a roadside come-on for a now defunct tourist shop by some entrepreneur who did not know or did not care that real tepees never had existed within hundreds of miles of this spot. Here is excellent material for high irony, but Klett has treated it gently, allowing us to feel the beauty as much as the sadness of the place. Among today's photographers of the West perhaps only Robert Adams, a guide for them all, has shown such generosity of spirit.

Klett has said that he wants more than to show us the grand landscapes and curious artifacts that he finds, and to evoke their histories, short and long. He wants us to feel that we are on the trip with him, participants in the search, tourists on an excursion. This most of all is what distinguishes Klett's pictures from the old survey photographs of the West. It always may seem, indeed may be true, that O'Sullivan and Jackson worked uncommonly hard for their views. Nevertheless Klett has shown that good pictures can also be made out of pleasure, and has shared his pleasure with us.

Traces of Eden: Travels in the Desert Southwest
was edited by Constance Sullivan
and designed by Katy Homans.
Production was supervised by Robert McVoy
and coordinated by Abigail Hutchinson.
The book was printed by Acme Printing Company, Medford, Massachusetts,
and bound by A. Horowitz & Sons, Fairfield, New Jersey.
The type, Monotype Fournier, was set by
Michael & Winifred Bixler, Skaneateles, New York.
Prints for reproduction were provided by Pace/MacGill Gallery, New York, New York.